Contents

Teachers' notes

The aim of the activities in this book is to support the implementation of the National Curriculum (January 1995) for geography at Key Stage 2. These activities should not be seen as teaching tools in themselves, but as opportunities for children to develop newly-acquired knowledge and skills. To maximise their benefit and to focus on the key aspects of the activity, it is important to explain carefully the purpose of each activity to the children before they begin. It would be useful also to have a display of photographs of river features, such as waterfalls, meanders, ox-bow lakes and deltas, around the classroom. Similarly, why not set up a display of Ordnance Survey maps (1:50000 and 1:25000) showing river features as well as a set of up-to-date atlases? This will enable the children to make links between streams and rivers in the UK and in other parts of the world.

The aims of this book

The aims of this book are:

- to introduce children to some of the terminology used in the study of rivers, such as 'source', 'mouth' and 'tributaries';
- to introduce some key features of rivers and streams, such as waterfalls, meanders and deltas;
- to describe how rivers erode, transport and deposit material;
- to examine some of the types of fieldwork that can be carried out at rivers and streams;
- to examine some of the important ways in which rivers interact with people, settlement, weather and the environment;
- to link river studies with map work.

Geographical content

The designation of Rivers as one of the four thematic studies in the revised National Curriculum (January 1995) has focused attention on rivers as key features of the landscape.

Rivers are important in a number of ways:

- **They shape the land's surface.** Every year they erode, transport and deposit billions of tonnes of rocks, soil and mud, and the processes by which rivers carry out these tasks determine the nature of the resulting landscape features. The Key Stage 2 programme of study states:

  In studying rivers and their effects on the landscape, pupils should be taught:

  a that rivers have sources, channels, tributaries and mouths, that they receive water from a wide area, and that most eventually flow into a lake or the sea;
  b how rivers erode, transport and deposit materials, producing particular landscape features, *for example, valleys, waterfalls.*

- **They have important effects on people, their lives and the places in which they live.** For example, very early settlers always looked to build their homes close to a river for a water supply, but on slightly higher ground to escape the dangers of flooding. Similarly many towns grew up at places where two or more rivers met, because rivers were important highways of trade and movement. Rivers have had important effects on many other aspects of people's lives too, such as finding the best place to build a bridge across a river (for example, Tower Bridge in London) or using a river valley for roads or railway lines to cross a range of mountains. In this context there are opportunities for you to link teaching about rivers with both thematic and place studies – the original sites of many **settlements** are closely linked to rivers; river floods are linked to **weather** such as heavy rain or snow melt; and, pollution of rivers is part of the **Environmental change** theme.

- **In school, rivers and streams provide good opportunities for developing children's fieldwork skills through firsthand investigations** (see pages 22, 23 and 24). As detailed in the programme of study for Geographical skills in the National Curriculum, such investigations will allow children the opportunity to:

a observe and ask questions about geographical features and issues;
b collect and record evidence to answer the questions;
c analyse the evidence, draw conclusions and communicate findings.

In particular the activities on pages 25–28 cover section 3d of the programme of study, dealing with the detail of Maps A, B and C.

Notes on individual activities

Page 5 : A river system

Aims: To introduce children to basic geographical terminology related to rivers, such as 'source', 'meander', 'mouth' and 'delta', and to help them to see the cyclical nature of rivers from source to sea.
Extension: Get the children to identify the different ways in which people interfere with river systems, such as extracting water for power stations, for towns or for irrigation as well as pouring industrial, domestic and agricultural waste into the system.

Page 6: How rivers work

Aim: To enable children to understand some of the processes by which rivers erode the landscape. While the emphasis is on erosion, reference is also made to transport of material. Deposition is dealt with in the next activity, but you may want to highlight the three interrelated processes of erosion, transport and deposition at this point.
Extension: Working in groups, ask the children to pour water from a watering can over a small mound of soil, sand and pebbles in the playground. Tell them to record how the water erodes, transports and deposits the material.

Page 7: Waterfalls

Aims: To help children see how a major feature of a river is formed and how the river processes produce changes in the height and shape of the waterfall. The activity is also designed to help children to make links between waterfalls in the UK and those in other parts of the world.
Extension: Encourage the children to write poems about waterfalls, especially their spray, their power and the roar of the water.

Page 8: Niagara Falls

Aims: To introduce a world-famous example of a major waterfall and to help children to make comparisons with waterfalls in other parts of the world. Highlight the problem of having an international frontier along the line of a river and its waterfall. The activity also involves using co-ordinates to label a diagram.
Extension: Let the children study an atlas map of the area and draw a simple sketch map to show: Lake Erie, Lake Ontario, the Niagara River and Niagara Falls, together with the surrounding towns such as Buffalo, Toronto, Rochester, Cleveland, Toledo, Detroit and Hamilton.

Page 9: Meanders

Aims: To show how rivers change course and create large bends called 'meanders'. In particular, the activity focuses on the processes of erosion and deposition within the meander and how they are related to the shape of the meander and the speed of flow of the river. Encourage discussion on the best way to measure the length of the course of the river from A to B. A piece of string or cotton laid around each curve and then measured against the scale will give the accurate distance. The open-ended nature of this labelling activity will allow differentiation by outcome. The sheet can be used with children of different abilities as the diagram boxes can be completed to varying levels of detail.
Extension: Get the children to study 1:50 000 OS maps to locate examples of rivers with meanders and to draw sketch maps of them.

Page 10: Ox-bow lake

Aim: To show how an ox-bow lake is formed and the river processes which affect its shape and development. The activity should help children to see how erosion and deposition by a meander creates an ox-bow lake as the river changes its course. Finding world-wide examples of meanders and ox-bow lakes is a useful way to develop the activity.
Answers: A=4; B=3; C=1; D=2.
Extension: The children can study 1:50 000 OS maps to find examples of ox-bow lakes on rivers with meanders.

Page 11: The valley side

Aim: To show how land use changes up the side of a valley. The activity is designed to help children see the three main parts of a valley (bottom, lower and upper slopes) and how the steepness of the sides affects land use and settlement.
Extension: Let the children use pictures of the valley sides along the River Rhine to help them to draw similar diagrams of how land use changes up the sides of the Rhine valley from the motorway and railway in the valley bottom through the vineyards to the castles on the upper slopes.

Page 12 and 13: Along the river – 1 and 2

Aim: To show how the characteristic features of a river valley change at different points along its course. The first sketch of a narrow, steep-sided valley is typical of a river in the hills or mountains. The second sketch shows a river which has eroded a wider valley with a flat floor and meanders.
Extension: Show the children pictures of rivers in their lower courses, near to the sea, and encourage them to use these as the basis for a third sketch to show how a river changes along its course.

Page 14: River flood

Aim: To use the example of the Lynmouth flood disaster as a case study of the causes and effects of a river flood. The resulting creative writing should emphasise the unexpected nature of the disaster.
Extension: Ask the children to collect newspaper clippings about floods in the UK and around the world and compare them with the Lynmouth disaster.

Page 15: Deltas

Aims: To describe how deltas are formed and to examine the ways in which people use deltas. The activity also encourages the children to identify deltas on rivers in other parts of the world.
Extension: Using reference books, the children can compare how different deltas are used, for example the Nile delta, Rhine delta and Mississippi delta.

Page 16: Rivers and settlement – 1

The site of a settlement

Aim: To highlight the links between the sites of settlements and river features such as defence, fording or bridging points on rivers.
Extension: Get the children to study maps of the sites of UK cities such as Durham, London and Birmingham and to identify the possible influence of rivers and streams.

Page 17: Rivers and settlement – 2

River ports

Aims: To highlight the importance of rivers to settlement, not just in terms of site, but as highways for trade and economic development. Many cities around the world began as river ports and the river is still an important feature of the city, for example London, New York, Rotterdam, Hamburg, Paris and New Orleans.
Extension: Ask the children to use an atlas to help them to compare two river ports such as London and Rotterdam. Get them to focus on the 'hinterland'; that is, the area from which each port draws its trade. The key features of the hinterland shown on an atlas map would be main cities, motorways, roads and railways, and whether the land is high or low-lying.

Page 18: Rivers at work

Aim: To highlight the importance of rivers to a wide range of human activities. Rivers are important not just for transport, but also for generating power, irrigation and as vehicles for waste disposal.
Extension: Together list the advantages and disadvantages of human activity along rivers. Which groups benefit (industry, cities, transport) and which can suffer (wildlife, local people)?

Page 19: A narrow escape

Aims: To help children realise some of the dangers of rivers and to understand the dramatic events which can take place along them. This activity should help children to develop their ideas in relation to creative writing.
Extension: The children could design and make posters to emphasise to other children and adults the dangers of playing near rivers.

Page 20: Water for crops, animals and people

Aims: To emphasise the importance of rivers in providing water for people, crops and animals. This activity also describes some of the ways in which water is stored then distributed to fields and homes.
Extension: Ask the children to make a list of as many ways as possible to save water in homes, schools, farms, factories and offices, for example, 'Turn it off!' campaigns.

Page 21: Polluting rivers

Aim: To show some of the main causes of river pollution in the UK and around the world.
Extension: Ask the children to imagine that they work on the local council. Which of the following activities would they allow on or around the reservoir and which would they forbid? In each case, discuss their reasons: fishing; swimming; water skiing; powerboat racing; picnic sites; and farming. Then the children could begin to suggest some possible solutions to the different types of pollution.

Page 22: Problems at the river

Aim: To show how conflicts of interest can arise between different groups who all want to use the

same resource. The activity can be used to show that some river uses are compatible, such as fishing and bird-watching, but others clearly are not.
Extension: Can the children suggest solutions to some of the conflicts? They may suggest, for example, using part of the river for activity sports and part for quiet sports, or separating activities at different times of the day.

Page 23: Building a reservoir

Aims: To examine some of the important factors of the upper parts of river systems and to relate the physical geography to human use. In this 'best location' activity the children select three possible sites and one best site for a reservoir. Most reservoirs are built in areas of high rainfall. Dams are placed where the valley sides are steep, and relatively close together so that the dam is as cheap to build as possible.
Extension: Get the children to think of the different ways in which a lake could be an asset to an area, for example, for wildlife or for water sports (windsurfing, fishing, yachting and so on).

Page 24: River map

Aims: To highlight the ways in which river features are shown on maps and to identify some of the key features. The activity is also a development of map work skills in relation to co-ordinates and symbols.
Extension: Ask the children to draw their own maps of river systems complete with a map grid and a key. Then get them to write instructions to enable a partner to draw the same map on a blank grid. They could colour in the maps appropriately.

Page 25: A river food web

Aim: To highlight the complex and delicate nature of food webs found in UK rivers. This activity has clear links with science yet relates closely to the use and abuse of rivers.
Extension: Using reference books, get the children to draw similar food webs for a lake found along the course of a river.

Pages 26 and 27: Stream survey – 1 and 2

Aim: These activities are to enable children to undertake fieldwork on streams (or rivers). The first two sheets can be used to gather general information about a stream (for example, in a local park or visited on fieldwork). It is probably best to divide the children into groups of three or four and spread them at points about 5–10m apart along the stream bank. In this way, each group is responsible for filling in the details about part of the stream. It also enables you to keep the group quite close together in the interests of safety and supervision.
Safety points: Children need to be reminded of the dangers of water and emphasis placed on responsible behaviour.

Some key points to remember are:

- Do not rush into the water. Stand on the bank and look.
- Not all the children need to go into the stream. They can take it in turns to do so, while the rest stand on the bank.
- All children should have plastic gloves when putting things in streams or taking them out because of the danger of Viles disease.
- Spare clothing is vital!
- Have as many responsible adults present as possible and explain what you want the children to do.
- Don't encourage the children to pick up 'polluting' objects such as broken glass – tell them just to record their positions.

Page 28: Measuring speed of flow

Aim: To measure the speed of flow. Tell two children to work together to clearly mark the start and finish of a 5m stretch on the bank of the stream. Get one other child to put an orange or a dog biscuit into the stream (these are heavy enough not to be blown about by the wind). Ask the children to time the orange/biscuit across the 5m distance and record this on the chart. Tell them to repeat this three times and then to find the average time.

Pages 29, 30 and 31: UK rivers, the River Rhine and the River Nile

Aims: To identify the locations and characteristics of rivers in the UK and to identify important towns along them and along two of the world's major rivers: the Nile and the Rhine. The activity is closely linked to the development of atlas skills and to Maps A, B and C in the National Curriculum programme of study.
Extension: Ask the children to use atlases to locate and map other major rivers such as the Danube, Elbe, Mississippi and Hwant-Ho together with their important cities.

Page 32: The World

Aim: To revise the names and locations of key rivers, together with other important geographical features (also specified in the programme of study) such as continent names, ocean names, cities, mountain ranges and countries.
Extension: Get the children to complete a similar activity, but only for the countries of Europe. Alternatively, use the map as the basis of a game. Write the names of the listed rivers, countries and cities on pairs of cards and use them to play 'Pairs' or 'Snap'.

See inside back cover for links to Scottish 5–14 Guidelines and Northern Ireland Curriculum.

● Name ______________________________

A river system

This diagram shows a pattern of streams and rivers joining together.
This is a river system from the hills to the sea.

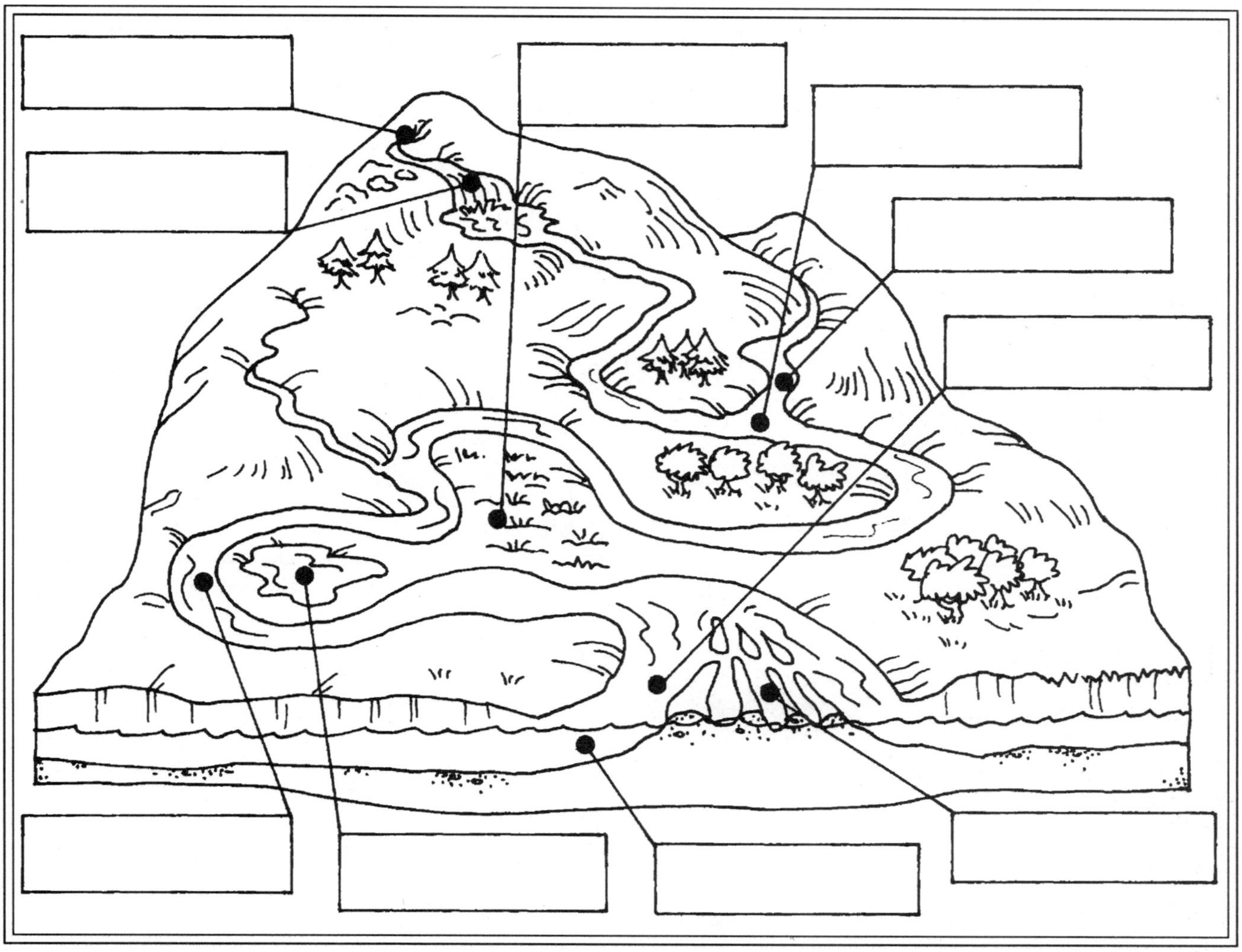

source	**confluence**	**mouth**	**lake**	**flood plain**
tributary	**waterfall**	**delta**	**meander**	**sea**

- Fill in the labels using the words below the diagram.
- Use the diagram to help you to fill in the gaps in these sentences:

• The place where a stream starts is called the ______________________.

• A ______________________________ is where two rivers meet.

• The ______________________________ is where the river enters the sea.

• The bends in a river are called __________________________________.

• ________________________ are triangular in shape and form where a river enters the sea or a lake.

● Name ______________________________

How rivers work

Streams and rivers always flow downhill. They carry with them loose rocks, pebbles and stones which knock against the sides (banks) and bottom (bed) of the river. This goes on for thousands of years and in time the banks and bed of the river are worn away. This wearing away is called **erosion**.

The diagram below shows how rivers move (**transport**) the rocks, sand and pebbles they pick up.

● Fill in the labels on the diagram using the words below:

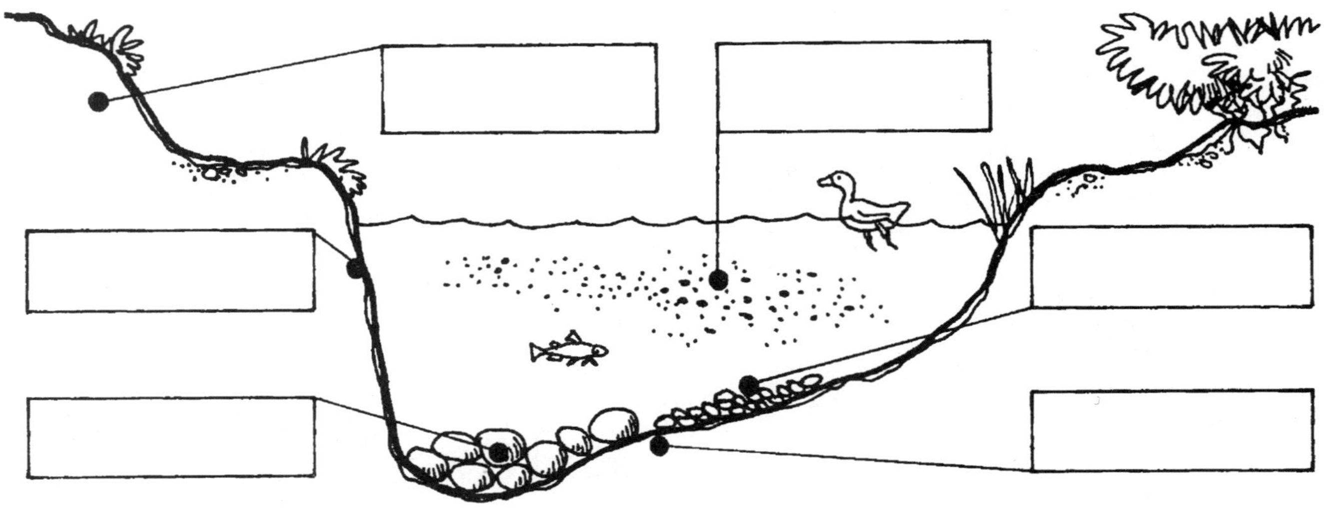

river bank **valley side** **small pebbles**
river bed **large boulders** **tiny rock pieces**

● In the chart below, tick the boxes to show which size of rocks you think could be moved along (transported) by each river.

River \ Rocks	Large boulders	Small pebbles	Tiny rock particles
In a slow-moving river			
In a fast-moving river			
In a flood			

● Use reference books to find out more about how rivers erode the land and the features they create, such as waterfalls and potholes. List two other landscape features created by rivers:

1 ______________________ 2 ______________________

● Name ______________________________

Waterfalls

Waterfalls form when a river plunges over the edge of a steep drop. The falling water crashes down to the river below.

Where are waterfalls found?

Waterfalls are found along rivers where hard rock lies above soft rock. The softer rock can be worn away by the river but the hard rock is left as a ledge over which the water falls. The pool at the bottom of the waterfall is called a **plunge pool**.

● On the diagram fill in the labels from the list below:

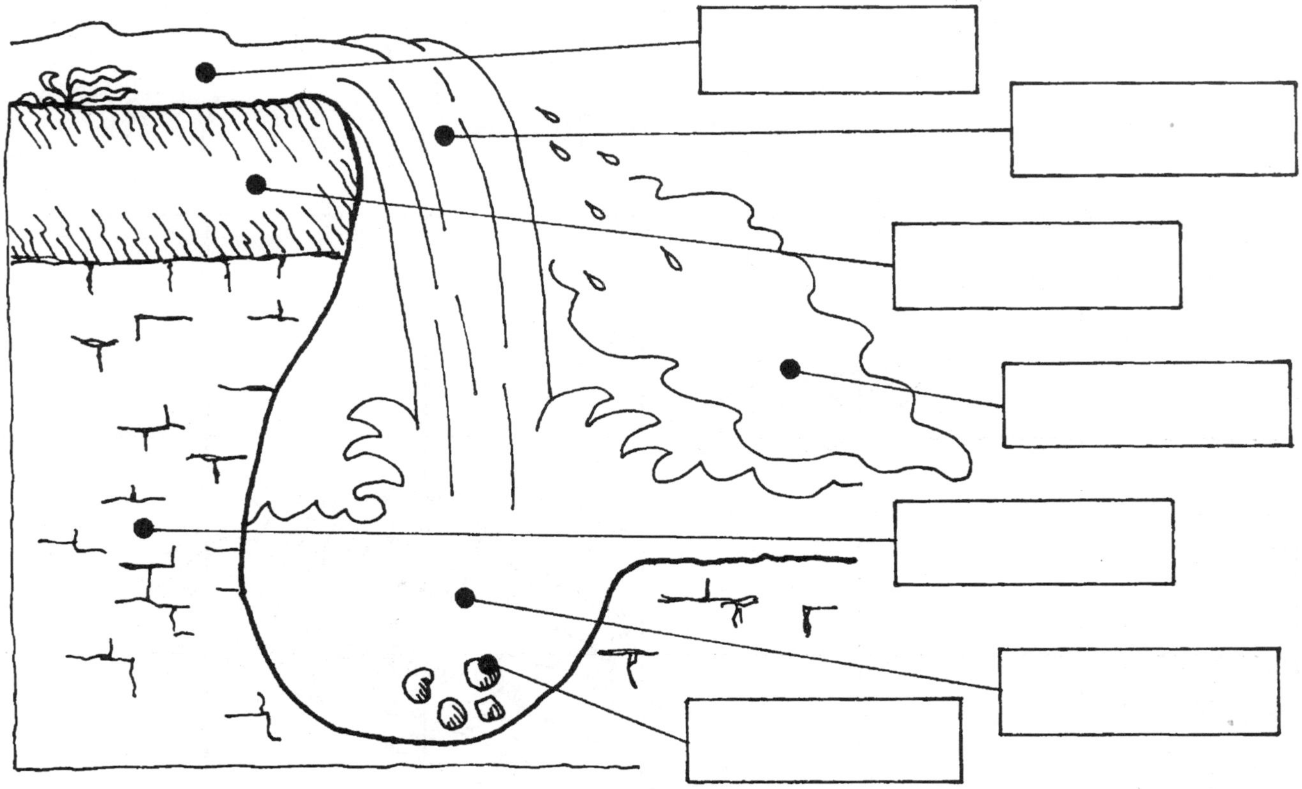

hard rock	**soft rock**	**plunge pool**	**waterfall**
spray	**river**	**rocks in the river**	

● Use an atlas and reference books to find and name:

- a waterfall in the UK ______________________________
- a waterfall in North America ______________________________
- a waterfall in Africa ______________________________
- a waterfall in Europe (outside the UK) ______________________________
- Which of these waterfalls is the highest? ______________________________

● Name ______________________________

Niagara Falls

● Complete the drawing of Niagara Falls, a major waterfall on the border of the USA and Canada, by adding these labels in the correct squares of the grid:

- Niagara River – B4;
- Horseshoe Falls – E3;
- Canada – D4 and E1;
- American Falls – D2 and D3;
- Gorge – C1;
- Goat Island – E3;
- USA – B3;
- Lake Erie – A4 and B4.

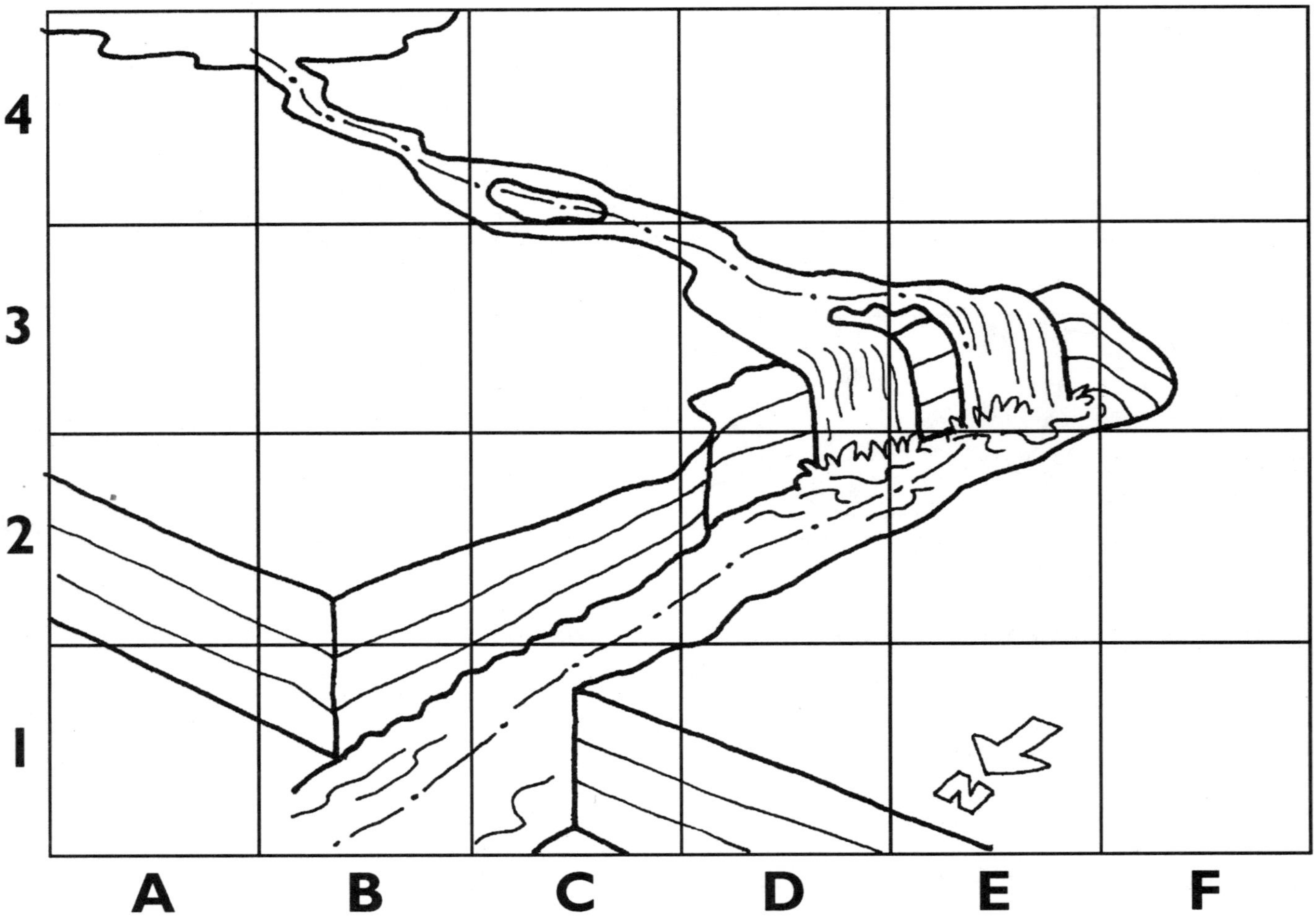

● Shade the three rock types in different colours.

● The dotted line shows the international frontier. Shade Canada in red and the USA in green.

● Name ______________________

Meanders

The shortest distance between two places is a straight line.

The map below shows part of the River Menderes in Turkey. As you can see the river has lots of bends in it. These bends are called **meanders**. They mean that a boat sailing from A to B has to go a long way round.

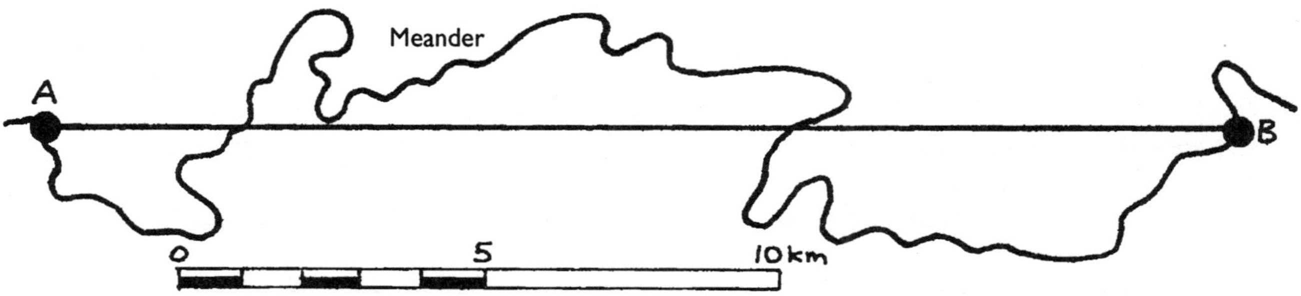

● How far is the straight line distance between A and B?

● How far is it between A and B following the river meanders?

This diagram shows what happens to rivers at meanders. Where the river is fast flowing it wears away the bank. Where the river is flowing slowly it leaves (deposits) sand, mud and pebbles.

● Use this information to complete the two boxes below (A and B) to explain how meanders develop.

Box A
Water is flowing fast on the outside of the meander, so ...

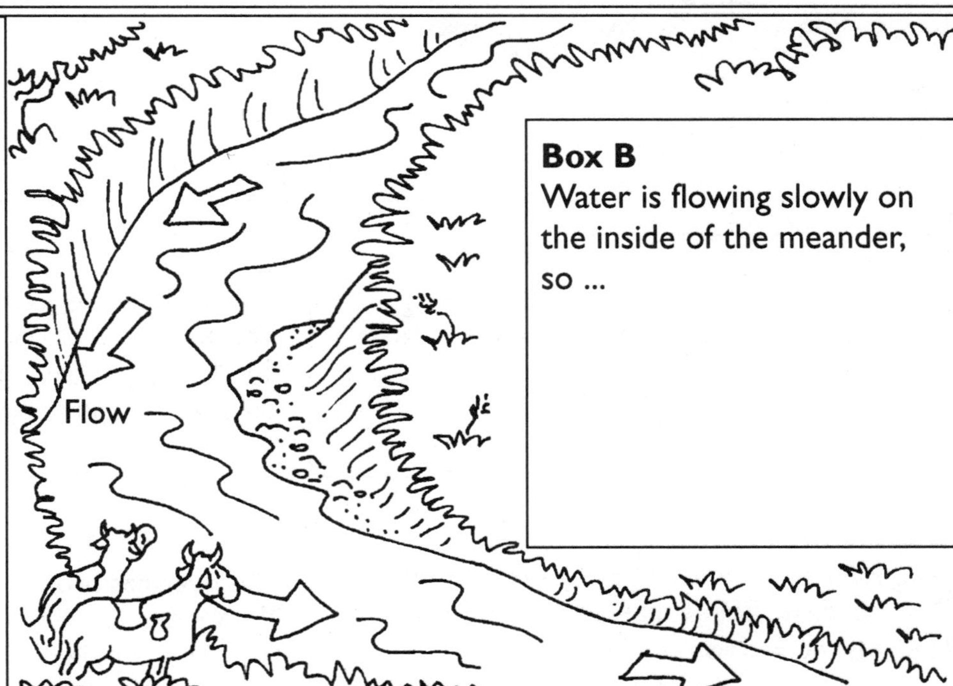

Box B
Water is flowing slowly on the inside of the meander, so ...

● Name ______________________________

Ox-bow lakes

These diagrams show how ox-bow lakes are formed, but they have been muddled up.

● Study the diagrams and cut them out. Stick them in order on to another piece of paper.
● Now cut out the written descriptions and stick the correct one under each diagram.
● Look in an atlas and see if you can name:

- a river with ox-bow lakes in the UK ______________________________
- a river with ox-bow lakes in Europe ______________________________
- a river with ox-bow lakes in the USA ______________________________

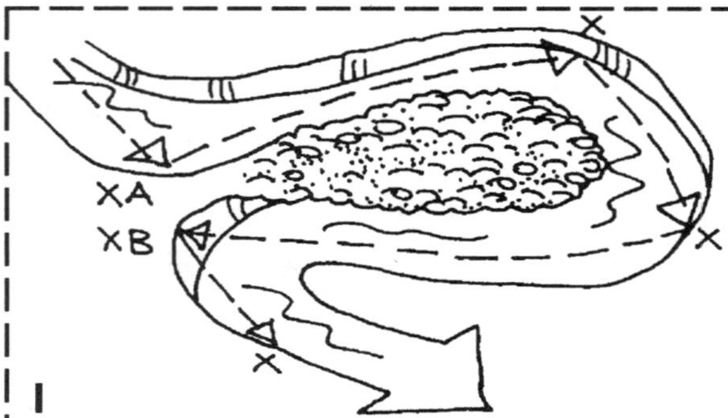

1

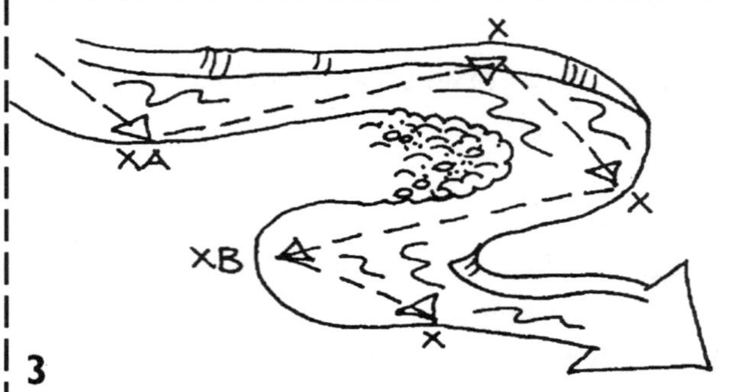

3

2

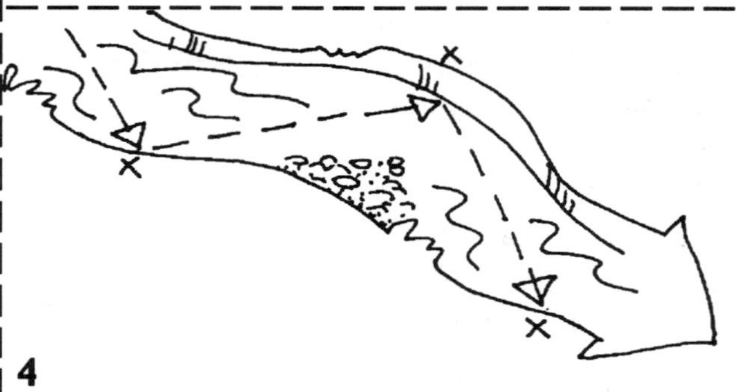

4

A
At this stage the river does not have a big meander. The river is wearing away the land at points X. On the inside of the meander the river is flowing slowly and deposits sand, gravel and mud.

C
By this stage the river has formed a huge loop. There is still erosion at all points X. During a flood time the river threatens to break through the gap between points XA and XB.

B
The meander starts to get more curved. The river is still wearing away (eroding) the land at all the points marked X. At points XA and XB the erosion is very fast.

D
The river has broken through between points XA and XB and left the meander as a cut-off lake. This is called an ox-bow lake.

● Name ____________________________

The valley side

The diagram below shows one side of a valley in the Lake District. It shows how the slope, land use and settlement change up the valley side.

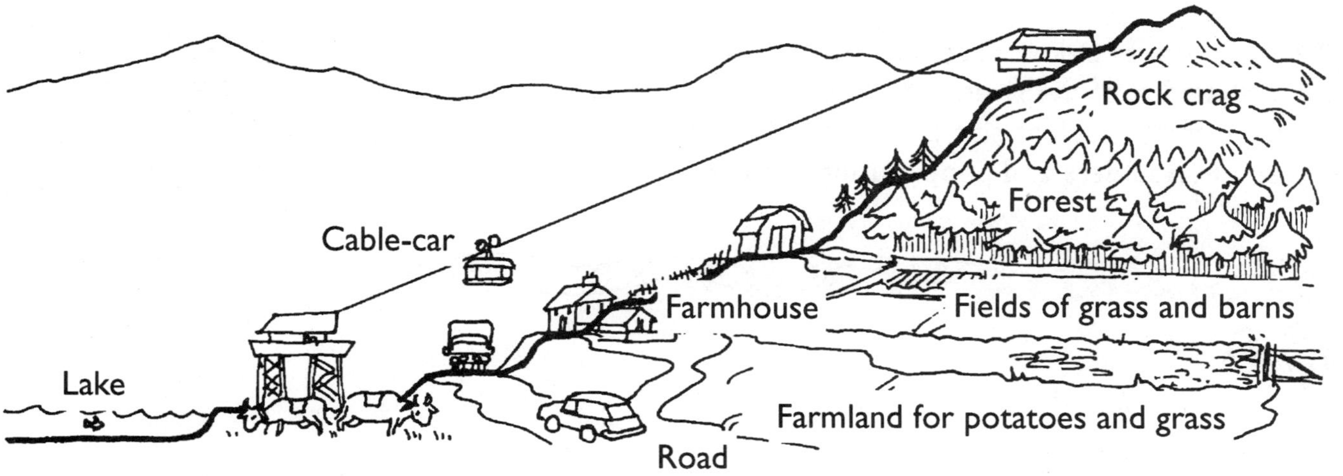

● Look carefully at the diagram then complete the table below. Part of it has been done for you.

	Valley bottom	Lower slopes	Upper slopes
Land use		Fields of grass	
Settlement	Farmhouse		No settlement
Slope		quite steep slope	

● Now imagine that you are riding on the cable-car up the mountainside. In each box describe all the things (farms, fields, crops, roads, trees) you would see on the valley bottom, then on the lower slopes and, finally, on the upper slopes. Continue on the back of this sheet, if you wish.

I can see the following things from the cable car:

Valley bottom	
Lower slopes	
Upper slopes	

● Name ______________________________

Along the river – 1

The pictures on the page 'Along the river – 2' show the start and a later stage of a journey down a river.

● Imagine you are floating over the river in a hot-air balloon and looking down on these stages of the river.

● In the boxes below, describe what you see (a) at the start of the river, and (b) lower down the river. Mention things such as size and width of river, river banks, waterfalls, boulders and people using the river.

A

B

Name ______________________

Along the river – 2

Name ______________________________

River flood

Look at this picture of Lynmouth after the devastating flood in 1952 and read how someone described what happened.

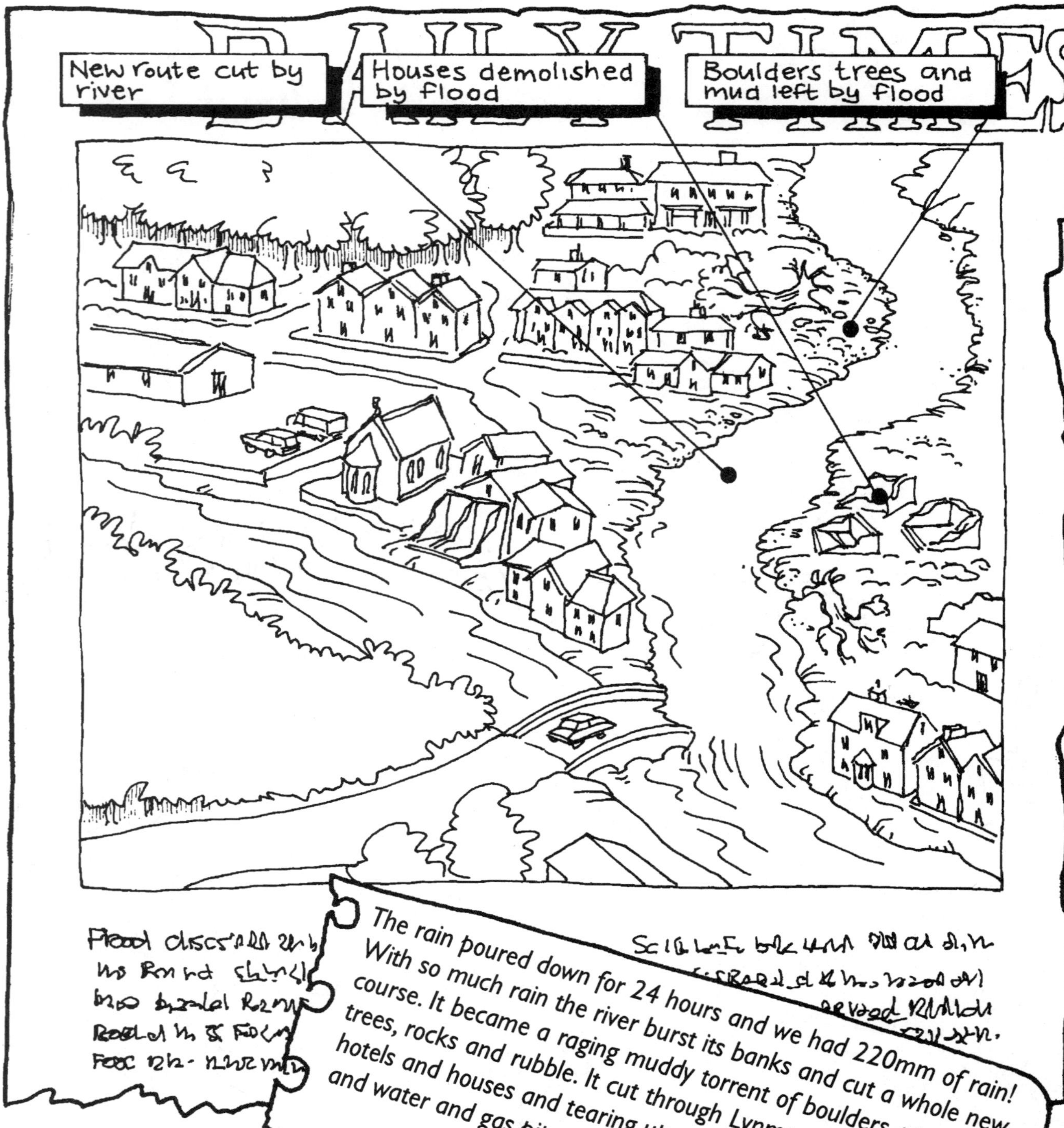

The rain poured down for 24 hours and we had 220mm of rain! With so much rain the river burst its banks and cut a whole new course. It became a raging muddy torrent of boulders, uprooted trees, rocks and rubble. It cut through Lynmouth, demolishing hotels and houses and tearing up roads and bridges. Power lines and water and gas pipes were washed away.

Imagine that you were in Lynmouth when the flood struck. Write a story describing what you saw and heard and how you felt. Explain what damage the river did and how you escaped from the floods. You could draft your ideas on the back of this sheet, if you wish.

Name ______________________

Deltas

When a river enters the sea or a lake it slows down. As the river slows down it dumps the sand and mud it has been carrying on the floor of the lake or sea. This sand and mud builds up over thousands of years to form new land called a **delta**.

- Look at this diagram of a delta on Lake Toba in Sumatra, Indonesia.
- Fill in the labels using the words below.

waterfall **river** **lake** **steep hillside** **forest** **village**

- How are the people using the delta?
- What dangers could people face living on a delta?
- How is the land of the delta different from the land behind it?
- Use an atlas and list some rivers with deltas in:

- the USA ______________________
- South America ______________________
- Africa ______________________

Name ______________________________

Rivers and settlement – 1

The site of a settlement

Many settlements were originally built close to rivers as these three pictures show.

- Cut out the descriptions. Stick the correct description below each picture.
- Give some more reasons why each site would be a good place to build houses.

A A small hill provides dry ground in a marshy area close to a river.

B A steep cliff with the river below provides a place safe from enemy attack for a settlement.

C This is the easiest point to build a bridge over the river. Several roads meet at the bridge so this becomes the site of a market.

- What were the advantages to early settlers of living near a river? What were the disadvantages?
- Look at a local map and find out what kind of site your village or town was built on.

● Name ______________________________

Rivers and settlement – 2

River ports

This picture shows a port on a major river such as the Thames, the Rhine or the Seine.

● Add the labels in the box to the picture.

jetty	river
oil storage tanks	helicopter pad
supertanker	road
cooling towers	electricity pylon
marshland	oil pipeline
deep water channel	railway
	power station

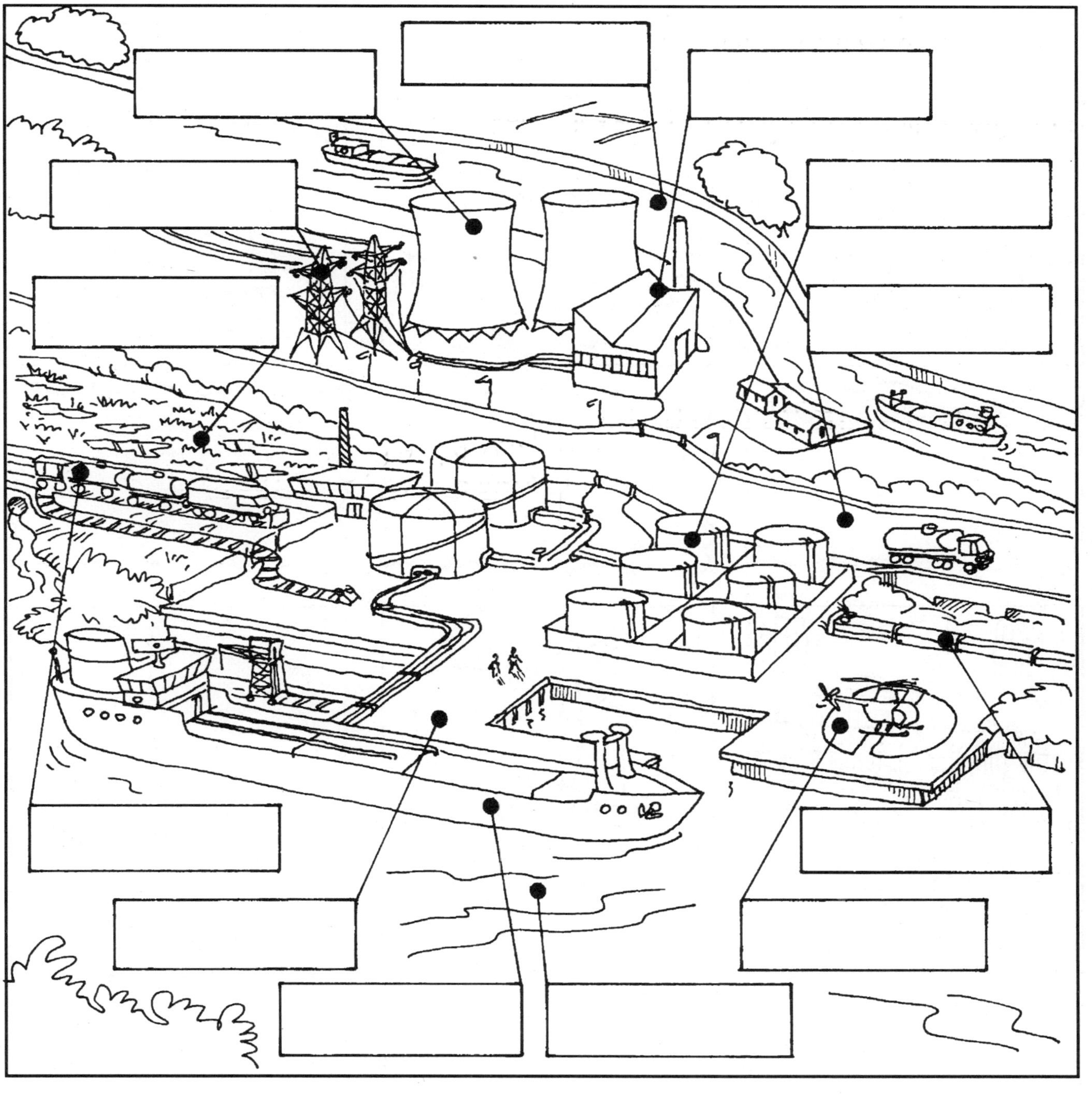

● Why do you think that the oil storage tanks are close to the jetty?

● Use an atlas and name as many towns as you can find which are river ports in Europe. List them on the back of this sheet.

● Why do river ports need lots of space?

● Name ____________________________

Rivers at work

Rivers are very useful in lots of ways.
The pictures below show some of these.

● Under each picture describe how the river is being used.

● In the empty box draw a picture of another way in which people use rivers and describe it underneath.

● Discuss which of these uses you consider to be good and which are bad.

• Name ______________________

A narrow escape

• Look at the pictures below.
They show the Walker family's day out on the river.

• Finish the story with another picture on the right below. Then write the full story on the left. You could continue on the back of this sheet or on another piece of paper.

● Name ________________________________

Water for crops, animals and people

● Complete rows 1 and 2 by drawing in the missing pictures.
● Complete the table by drawing pictures in row 3 to show the source of the water, how it gets to the fields and how it is used.

Description	Source of water	How water gets to fields	How water is used
1 In some places water is stored in reservoirs and sent in canals to water fruit trees			
2 In some places water from wells is pumped to the surface for animals to drink			
3 In some places water from reservoirs is sent in pipes to people's homes and gardens			

● Use the figures below to draw a bar graph on the back of this sheet to compare the water consumption in the different countries.

Water taken from the water cycle by some of the world's thirstiest countries	
Country	**Water for all uses per person per day**
Australia	3,330
Canada	4,140
France	1,380
Italy	2,700
Japan	2,540
Netherlands	2,740
Spain	2,660
UK	710
USA	6,330

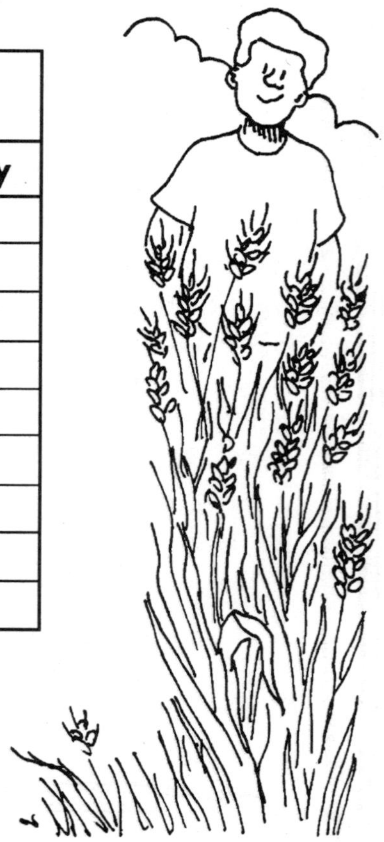

● Now answer these questions, using your graph to help you.
- Which country uses the most water per day?
- Which country uses the least?
- Can you explain the results?

● Name ______________________________

Polluting rivers

This drawing shows how rivers can sometimes be polluted.

● On the drawing mark:

- a blue circle where the river is not polluted;
- a red circle where the river is most polluted;
- a yellow circle where it would be safe to swim in the sea.

● On the back of this sheet describe how the river has been polluted.

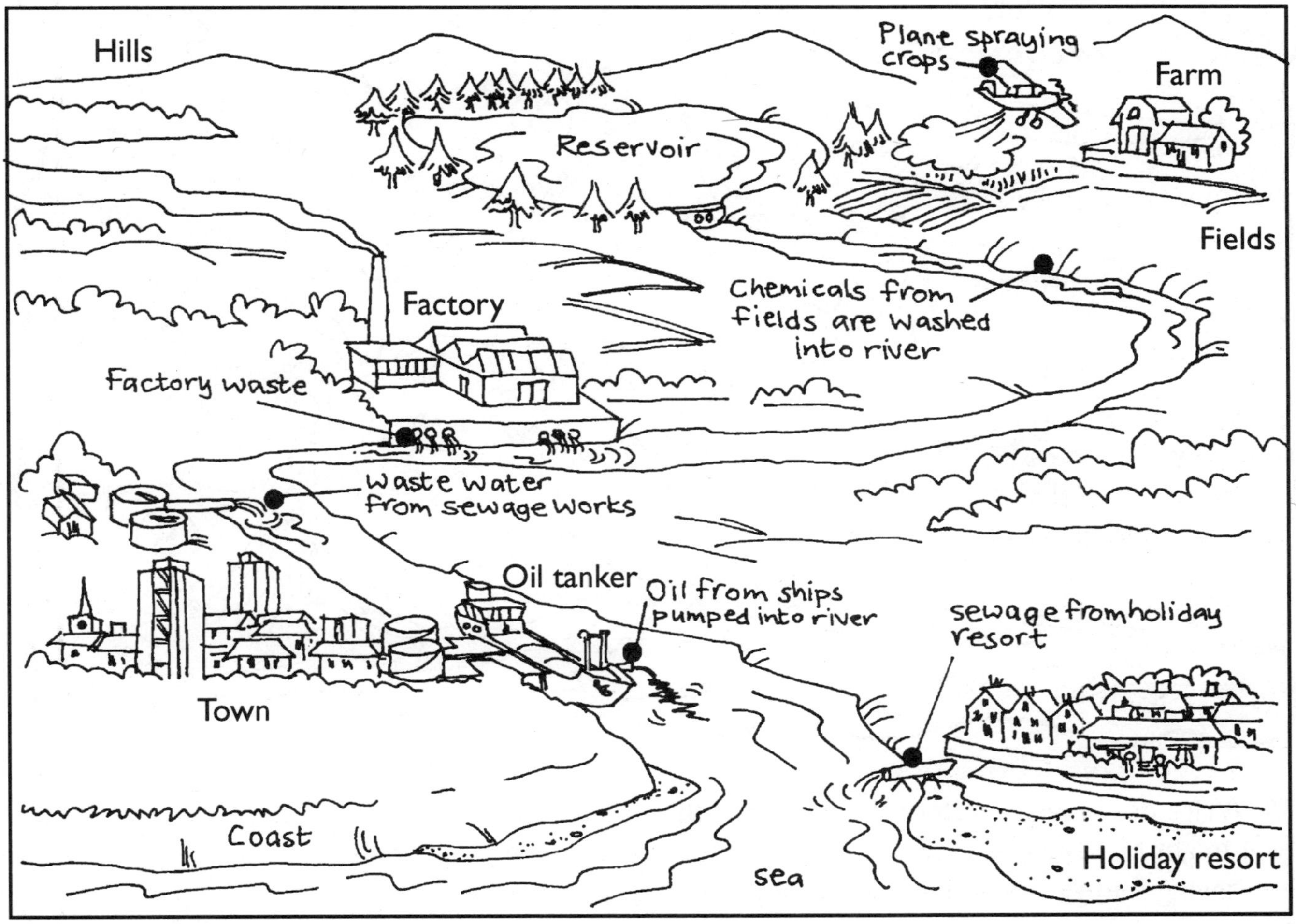

● Now imagine that the picture above shows your locality and finish this letter to the Editor of the local paper. In your letter point out the different types of pollution along the river and explain why they are dangerous:

The Editor
The Local Daily
Printer's Row
My Town

Dear Editor,
I am writing to warn other local people of the dangers in our beautiful river.

● Name ______________________________

Problems at the river

Lots of people like to spend a day out by a river and the picture below shows some of the activities that can take place. Unfortunately, some activities get in the way of others.

● Write down what each of the people in the drawings numbered 1 to 4 might be saying about what is happening. For example, the people in drawing 5 might be saying: 'I wish they would turn down their radio or go somewhere else.'

1 ______________________________

2 ______________________________

3 ______________________________

4 ______________________________

● On the back of this sheet, make a list of all the activities you can see in the picture. Add to your list any other activities you can think of that take place on rivers, such as paddling or bird-watching.

● Which of the activities in your list would you like to be doing?

● Which of the activities cause most pollution?

● Name ______________________

Building a reservoir

As the drawing below shows, the upper parts of rivers are often in deep, steep-sided valleys.

● Imagine that a water company wants to build a dam in this area to create a reservoir. Pick three places where dams could be built and mark the dams on the drawing in red, green and yellow. Shade in blue the areas that would be flooded behind each dam.

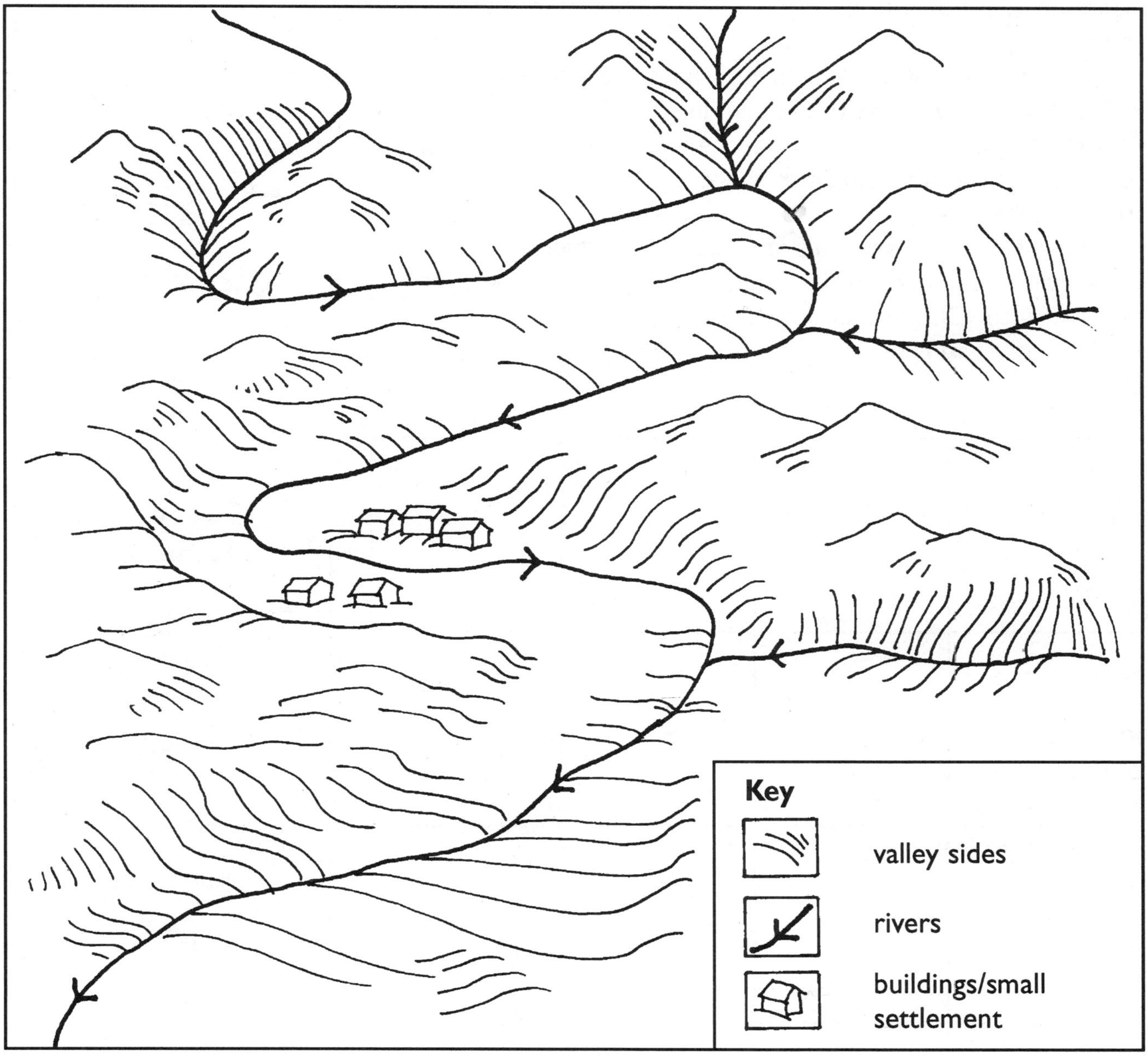

● Which would be the best site for a reservoir? Why? ______________________

____

● Do you think that farmers and local people would be in favour of building the dam and the reservoir? Explain your answer. ______________________

____

____

● Name ______________________

River map

● Use the symbols in the key to draw this map:

- There is a sandy estuary which runs through C2 and D2.
- The main river runs from A4, and then has three meanders in A3. There is an island in the middle of one of these meanders. The river continues from A3 into B3 with one meander, then flows south into B2, and then east into the estuary in C2.
- A stream flows from A1, through B1, to join the main river in B2. There is a weir on the stream in A1.
- Another stream flows from a lake in C4, through B3, to a confluence with the main river. There is a footbridge over the stream in B3.
- There is a marshland on both sides of the river in A4.
- A major road runs from A2, into B2, across a bridge over the river into C3, and then into D4.
- A minor road runs from the main road in C3 south to the estuary in C2 where there is a car park.

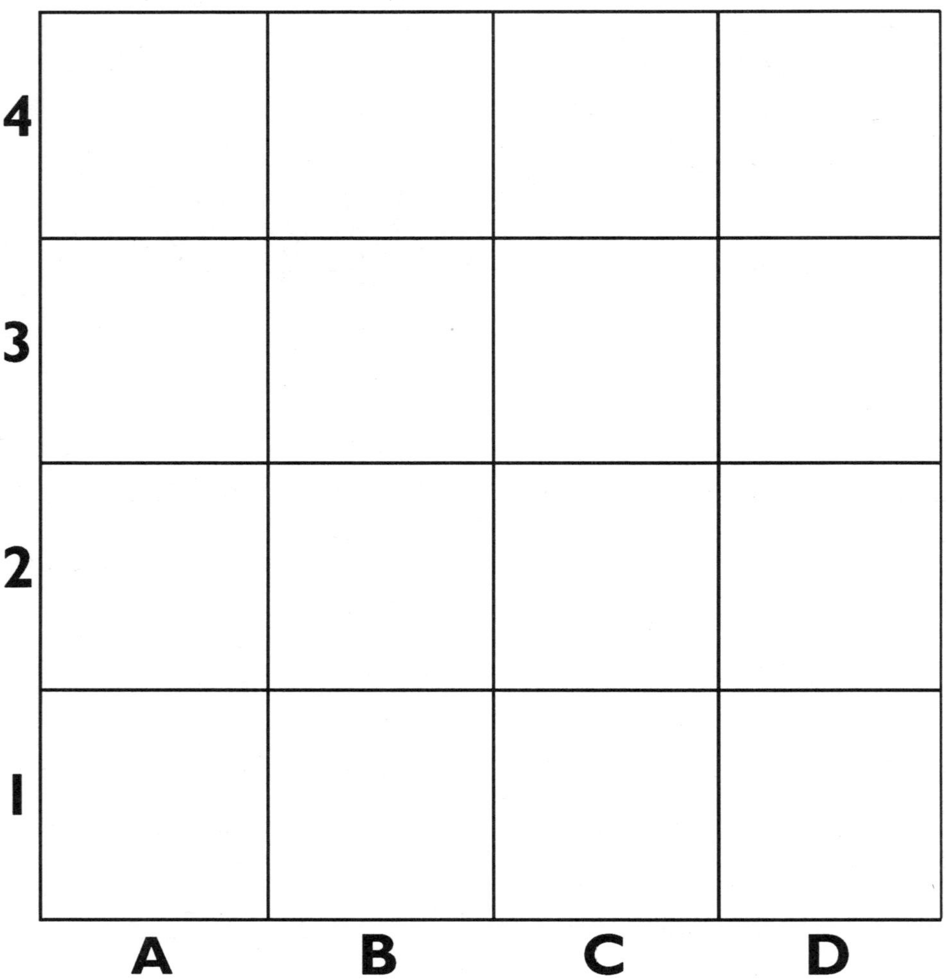

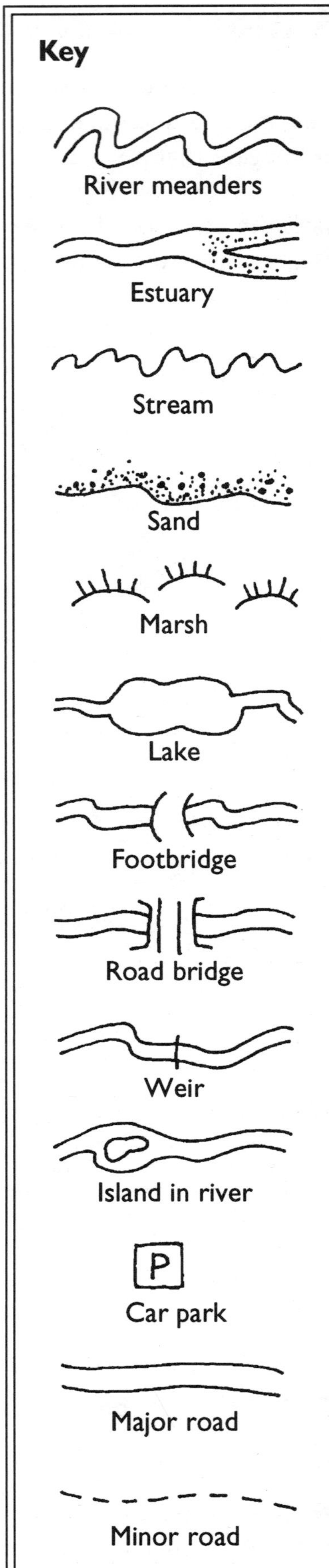

● Compare your finished map with a partner's. How are they similar or different?

● Name ______________________________

A river food web

In and around rivers there are lots of different insects, fish, birds and animals. The diagram below shows some of these. It is called a **food web** and shows how some creatures feed off others in rivers in the UK.

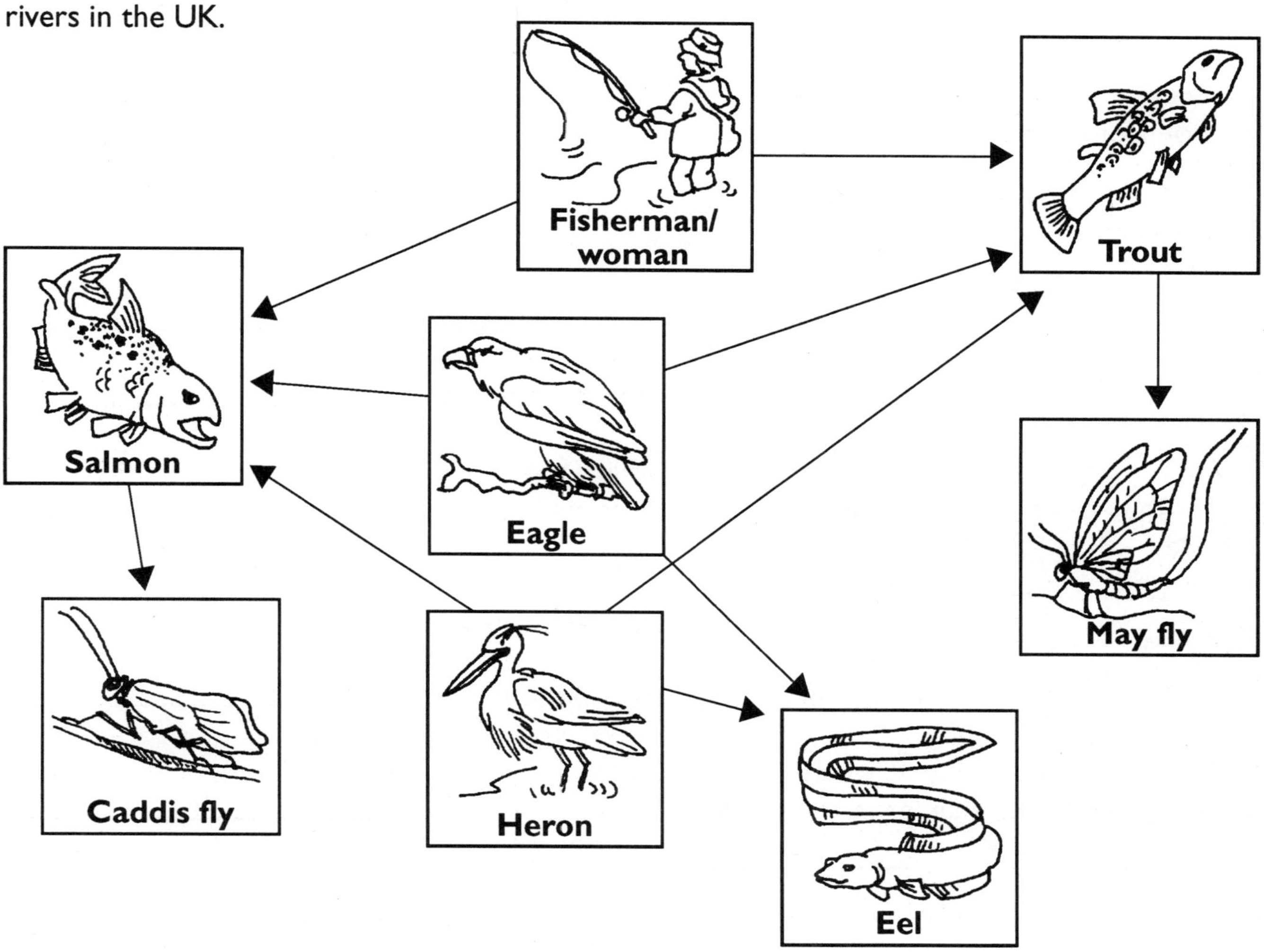

● Write down what each of these creatures eats:

- the eagle ______________________________
- the eel ______________________________
- the trout ______________________________
- the heron ______________________________
- the fisherman/woman ______________________________
- the salmon ______________________________

● What would happen if all the May and Caddis flies were destroyed? ______________________________

____

● What might kill them? ______________________________

____

● What would happen if the heron died? ______________________________

____

- Name ______________________

Stream survey – 1

Be careful near water

Date ______________

Name of stream ______________________________

Location of stream ______________________________

Position along stream bank ______________________________

Look at the stream

- What colour is the water? ______________________
- Are there plants growing in the stream? ______________________

If plants are growing where are they in the stream (for example, at the sides, or in the middle)? ______________________

____

- Is the stream straight or curved? ______________________
- Is there mud or sand in the stream? ______________________

- If there is mud and sand, where is it in the stream (for example, at one side, or in the middle)? ______________________

____

____

Look at the banks of the stream

- How high are the banks? ______________________

____

- Are the banks steeply sloping or gently sloping? ______________________

____

- What plants are growing on the banks? ______________________

____

- Is there any rock or soil exposed on the banks? If so, what colour is the soil? What texture is the soil? ______________________

____

____

● Name

Stream survey – 2

⚠ Be careful near water

Look at the depth of the stream

● If the stream is shallow use a ruler to measure how deep it is.

● How deep is it at each side?

● How deep is it in the middle?

Look for pollution of the stream

● Is the water clear or cloudy?

● Are there things thrown into the stream, such as cans or bottles?
If so, make a list of all the different things your can see.

● Where are the things thrown in the stream
(for example, at the sides, or in the middle)?

● In the space below, draw a sketch map of the stream to show:

- the shape of the stream;
- the position of plants;
- the position of any bridges and footpaths;
- the position of any rubbish;
- the position of any sand or mud in or near to the stream.

● Name ______________________________

Measuring speed of flow

⚠ Be careful near water

● Measure the time in seconds taken for the orange or dog biscuit to flow from A to B (5m).

● Enter the time in the first box.

● Do this again twice more. Find the average of the three times.

● Divide your average time by 5 to give the speed of flow in seconds per metre.

Speed of flow (time in seconds to flow 5m)				
Distance	**Test 1**	**Test 2**	**Test 3**	**Average time**
A to B				

Speed of flow = $\frac{\text{Average time}}{5}$ = seconds per metre

● Try the same test at two other places along the river. How does the speed flow vary between the three places.

● Name ______________________________

UK rivers

This map shows some of the main rivers in the UK.

● Use an atlas and name:

- **River Trent**
- **River Thames**
- **River Severn**

● Draw in and name as many of the following rivers as you can.

Would a key be useful?

- River Avon
- River Ouse
- River Wharfe
- River Aire
- River Nidd
- River Tywi
- River Dee
- River Teifi
- River Trent
- River Exe
- River Tees
- River Tyne
- River Wear
- River Usk
- River Bann
- River Tweed
- River Clyde
- River Forth
- River Dee
- River Lagan

● Name ______________________________

The River Rhine

The map shows the River Rhine and the countries it flows through.

● Use an atlas and name on the map countries 1, 2, 3, 4, 5 and Lake 6.
● Mark these towns along the River Rhine with a red dot and name them:

- Duisburg
- Düsseldorf
- Cologne
- Bonn
- Koblenz
- Mainz
- Heidelberg
- Strasbourg
- Basel

● Name the two seas 7 and 8.

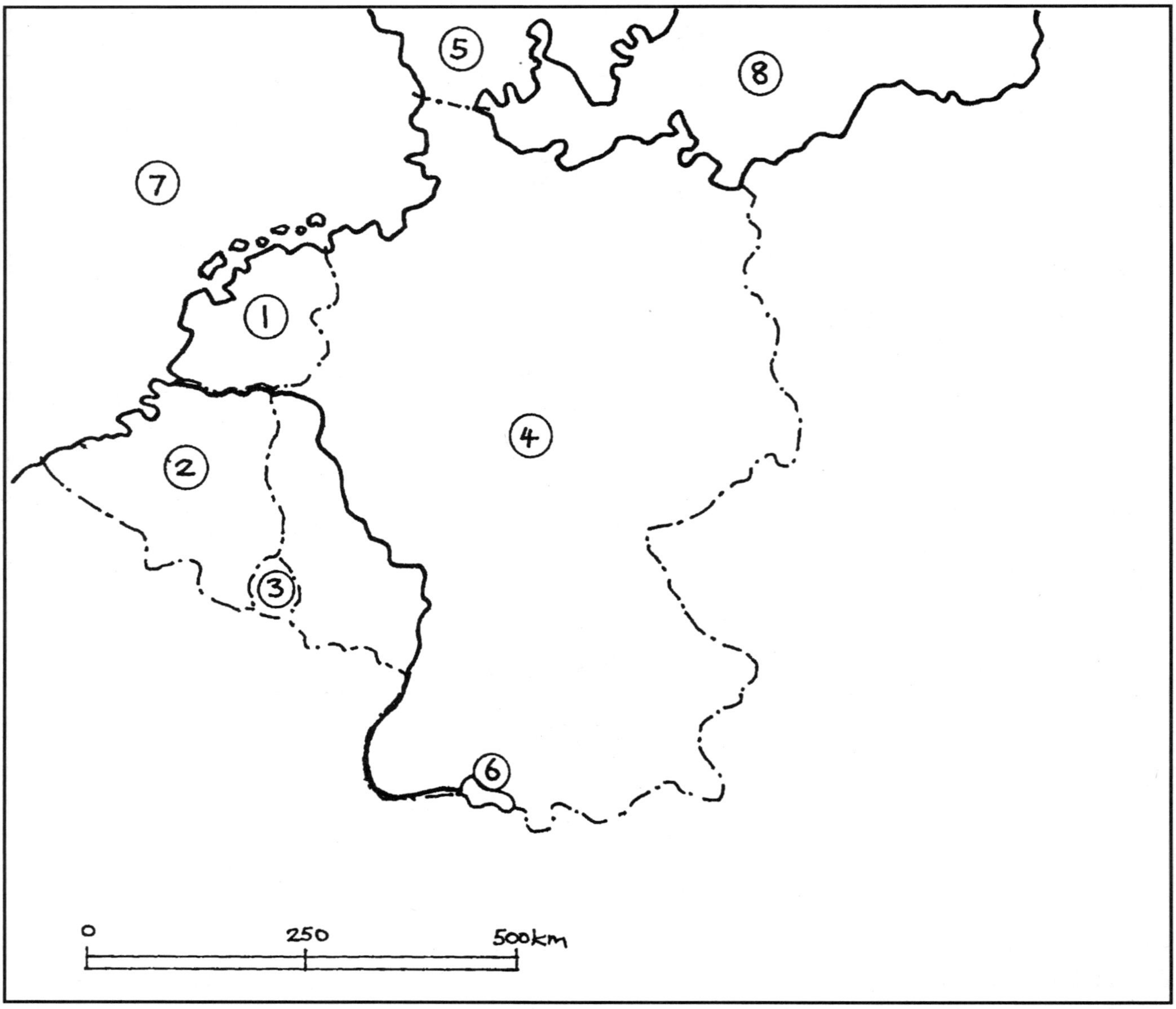

● Use reference books to find out as much as you can about the River Rhine. Compare it with:

- a river near to you;
- a river in another country, such as the River Nile.

● Name ______________________________

The River Nile

The map shows the River Nile in Africa.

● Use an atlas to mark on and name:

- Lake Tana
- Blue Nile
- White Nile
- Nubian Desert
- Mount Kenya
- Mount Kilimanjaro
- Red Sea
- Indian Ocean
- Libyan Desert
- Ethiopian Highlands

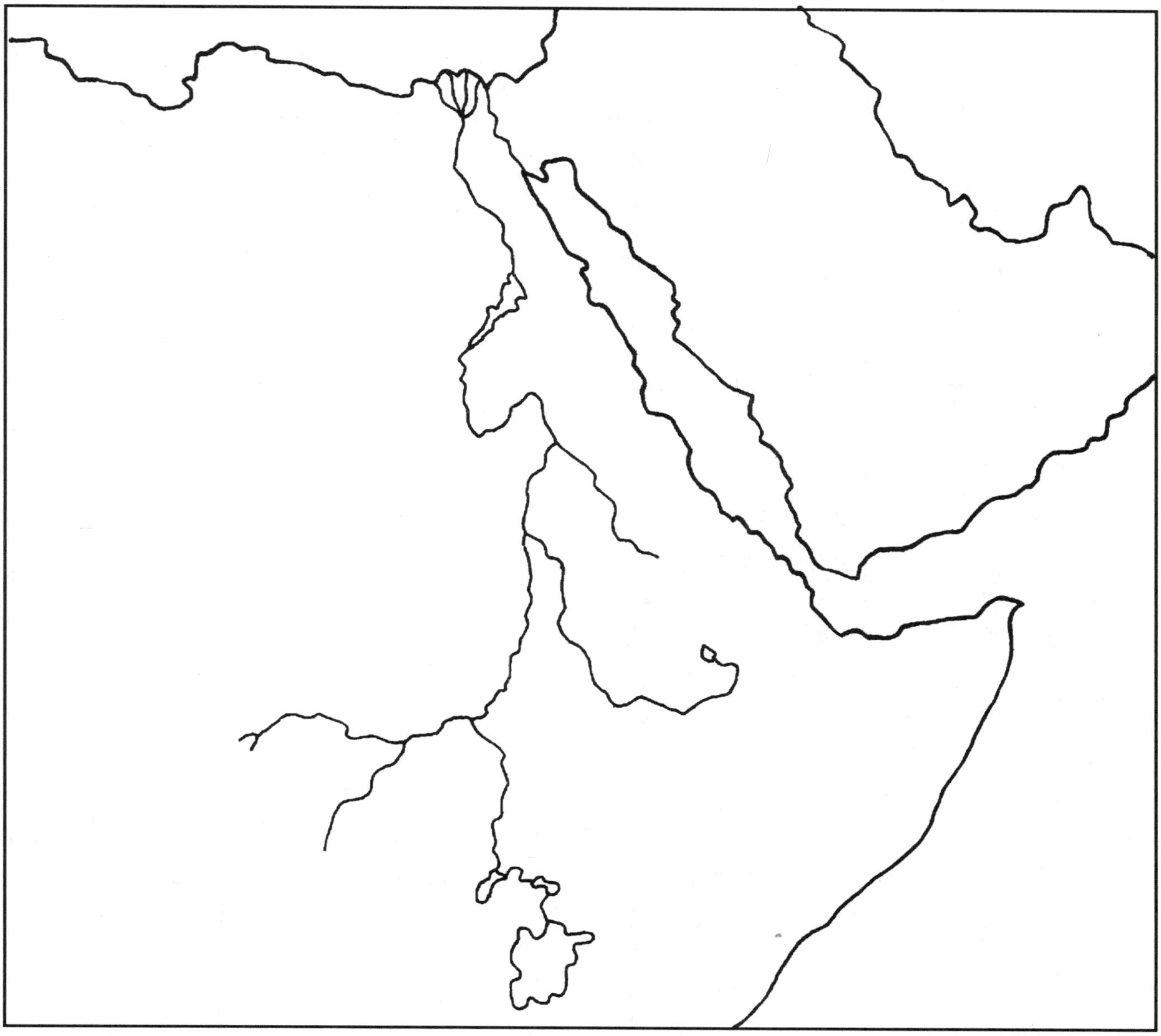

● Mark with a red dot and name Cairo, Alexandria, Aswan, Khartoum.

● Use an atlas and label the sea that the Nile flows into.

● Label the countries that the Nile and its tributaries flow through.

● Name the desert that the Nile crosses.

● Use reference books to find out as much as you can about the River Nile. Compare it with:

- a river near to you;
- a river in another country, such as the River Rhine.

The world

- Use an atlas to label as many of these things as you can on the world map:

- Pacific Ocean
- Atlantic Ocean
- Indian Ocean
- Arctic Ocean
- River Mississippi
- River Amazon
- River Nile
- Oceania
- Antarctica
- Africa
- North America
- South America
- Europe

- Mark these town with a red dot and name them:

- New York
- Buenos Aires
- Paris
- Cairo
- Bombay
- Sydney

- Label these countries:

- USA
- Canada
- Brazil
- Russia
- India
- China
- Australia
- Indonesia

- Colour these mountain ranges in brown and label them:

- Rocky Mountains
- Andes Mountains
- Himalayas

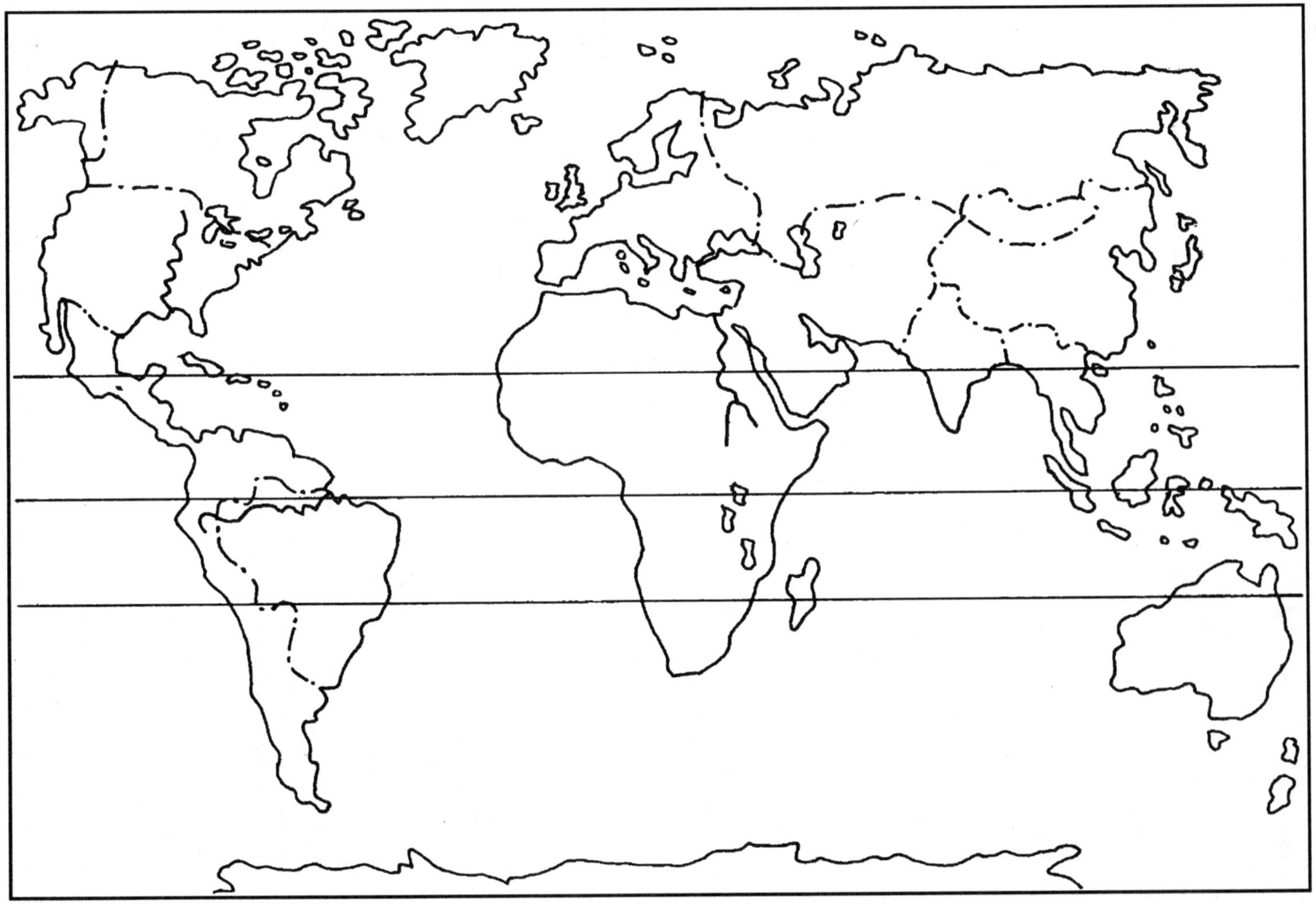